Praise for *Atmosphere of Mona*

As I read this book, I was making little notes to myself, and came across a piece of paper on which I'd written...'it consoles, sustains and restores.' Which indeed it does. It is a masterwork - from the opening majestic image to the closing one. It's a great flow of words, slowing, gathering pace, surging - as nature does. It provokes thoughts and anxieties, yet there is such joy and tenderness, a balm, 'a doorway of hope', with 'nature more determined than tarmac.' It is personal and profound, written by a man whose eyes and senses miss very little; would that I could experience all that Matthew Shaw does in his epic *Atmosphere of Mona*. – *Shirley Collins*

Matthew Shaw channels reverse traditions into the future via music/word gnosis, landscape as character/life, and a connection to the heart that is as direct, and spontaneous, as it is unerringly true. - *David Keenan*

He has turned to reveal but not reversed his language. Previously he spoke through a layered sound of landscape that moved through time. Horizontal drifting, entwining and layering cloud on earth, light on wind, weather as a pulse. Drawing out history as a surface without image, so that we might understand the flow through our listening hearts. That is what Matthew Shaw does in his music. What he is known for.

Now he casts individual notes as words. Verticals which he gently demands we pause to taste; seeds, pathways, gateposts and lenses. These poems hold space and breath in a Haiku of moments; the drift of the music cupped, stopping us dead in our tracks. Now the flow and ebb, which he mastered before, watches the singularity of the moment. The stand still to breath in the actual moment. The primal zen of now. – *Brian Catling*

Matthew Shaw is a magnificent voice of the nature spirit as well as the human spirit. He combines beautiful feelings with clear thoughts. I am always inspired by the depth of his powerful poems – *Satish Kumar*

The work combines autobiography, nature observation (let's say an acute awareness of things) and a precarious sense of the "other".

At first sight the lines themselves might seem plain, almost like diary notes. But in this unadorned directness there is in fact a lot of heft. In common with them, Shaw is able to give a sense of the mythic in the everyday. Even that word "mythic" is a bit too much of a burden though for something more intangible, but resonant. I think what these poems show is attentiveness, open-ness, a sensitivity to possibilities but without tipping over into anything too obviously pantheistic. There is an implied animism, perhaps, but even this might be understood as metaphorical. Reading them is a subtle experience, requiring reflection and extrapolation: walking with you just a few steps further on from what the lines actually say. - *Mark Valentine*

Atmosphere of Mona

Matthew Shaw

Published by Annwyn House in 2020
Derby, UK
annwynhouse.weebly.com

© Matthew Shaw, 2020

ISBN (Paperback): 978-1-9998683-2-1
ISBN (E-book): 978-1-9998683-3-8

The right of Matthew Shaw to be identified as the author of this work has been asserted by him in accordance with the Copyright, Designs and Patent Act 1988.

All rights reserved. This book is sold subject to the condition that it shall not, by way of trade or otherwise, be lent, resold, hired out or otherwise circulated in any form of binding or cover other than that in which it is published, and without a similar condition, including this condition, being imposed on the subsequent purchaser.

Cover photographs by Matthew Shaw
Cover design by Rupert Morrison

Dedication
To Marlene Shaw

Introduction

Atmosphere of Mona came to be from a conjunction of two thoughts. The first was based on a dream that I had while visiting Anglesey. Here my maternal grandmother, Mona Broughton, was with me in a vivid yet entirely domestic setting. Mona was rummaging through a drawer in the old cabinet, which was placed against a wall in my grandparent's living room. These drawers had an unfathomable and almost endless depth, containing paperwork, postcards, old letters, hair grips, pipe cleaners, old coins, a magnifying glass, and so on. In the dream Mona was looking for something but could not remember what. It was in there somewhere, and Mona would know when she found it.

It was like searching for a memory or a word, just on the tip of her tongue.

The second thought concerned my maternal great-grandmother, Mary Jones. Mary had lived in north Wales, but the details of her were scarcely remembered in our family. Mary had not moved far from her home in north Wales before settling in Cheshire. There was something about her that I connected with being on Anglesey. My trip there was to take photographs and make sound recordings. As I travelled, I spent an increasing amount of time in the rural and ancient places of the island.

I began to make connections with names and places. Anglesey's Welsh name is Ynys Môn. In Latin, this translates as Mona. A coincidence I liked the thought of. and it so became a maternal companion as I went about my travels.

I wanted to look deeper into the word Mona. I drew on my studies in Hebrew to do so.
מ   *Mem*; Central cause, creativity, symbol of woman and mother.
ו   *Vov*; Mother vowel O, the absolute, the point which separates nothingness and being.
נ   *Nun*; fruit, water, cause and effect.
Aleph; Mother vowel. The abstract principle of a thing, stability, continuity.

I drew also on folklore, etymology of the names of places and symbolic language, carvings in stone and landscape alignments.

The next morning, when I awoke, I decided I would write down each mornings dream. If I didn't dream, or couldn't remember a dream, I would mediate and write down what happened.

These dreams and mediations after one year formed the initial beginnings of this book. I spent the following year returning to what I had written, made amendments, revisiting the photographs I had taken. This process created what has now become the book you hold in your hands.

-Matthew Shaw, 2020
Christchurch, Dorset

Ingress

A beginning.

The clouds so begin.

Winter sun shining
I walk out into the water
worries dissolve into the endless horizon

The Memorial is still standing
circles of eternity
three times around.

Past, present & future
the earth temple
portal potential
element of fire
with towering landmarks

Earth inferno passes to air,
water reflection of abstract mind
until whenever reaching skywards,
to beyond earthly realms

Into the circle
outside of the tides of time
a gateway to forever
reframed experience

Beneath emerald canopy
mottled moonlit kisses

The piper through the gates of dawn
the sun runs itself in circles

Tidal lunar island
circumference of sea
cousin to the mainland
what was once is still to be.

Stone fortress walls
containing Eden
three hills

three stories
three perspectives
circle of sound, Yew tree dimension
a Meeting place, two streams combine
a central point
a stitch in time,

Lost and found
lost again to be found again
named and familiar
on sacred ground

Deep wooded shrine
immune to time
hedgerow wisdom
third sibling

Tidal cycle continues to flow
what remains
remains

A Circle of light
and a circle of stone
as a landlocked Island
the emerging future
a shining beacon
hidden depths

Table top treasure arrow
three-legged vision machine
Prehistoric solar layers
mist rising mythology
Tree lined expressionism
quest led nostalgia hive mind.

Remembrance fun-day
streets named after daughters,
playing on doorsteps
chalk smeared footsteps
Sweet wrapper archaeology

Recumbent clock face space station
high magic astral sundial
Fern fence of sentinels
the silent watcher,
watching with discernment
focused concentration
viewing from a higher place
always with detachment

White topped perfection
unmarked pathways
snow pyramid dreaming
in centre of the circle

Above the clouds
and the highest mountains.
back to earth the bluestone sentinels
their circular economy
vertical integration
horizontal now-space of simple bliss
landscape latitude, longitude logic.

Solar observatory
chlorophyll filter
oxygen giver

Soar over oceanic clouds
silhouetted coastal tomb
lone standing stone,
white hungry guardian
shackled and free only temporarily
A Mouth within the earth
stone shelf lichen
stream to lands end
through ancient storied lanes

To the horseshoe cove of dreams
circular dominance
building site history,
remembering visitors
visiting voyeurisms

Arched perspectives with hidden depths
discreet almost hidden
earth womb cave
overgrown pleasure
shrouded warmth

Spring of life
emerging flow
From hidden depths
crystal clear,
beyond the circles of time.
Endless trailing alleyways
portals to yesteryear
transported through grime
for those that can hear

Set still in stone
looking to heaven,
air deity temple
maps are not territories

Something for everybody
in this hidden ghost example.
elephant tree watching
arms spinning sun wise,
widdershins wanderings back to beginnings.

Black wall of evergreen
trees of light infusion
past all kinds of darkness
future light and optimism
coastal landscape sweep
bay of remembrance,
reflected soul searching
sky soaring sightline
flight of freedom
traveling upwards
beyond land and ocean

The returning dawn
arboreal landscape dreaming
gloamings of falling leaves
twilights under canopy
walking towards things unseen but felt
midnight forest footpath
disappearing into darkness

Lit by determination
tomorrow a smile away
familiar trees revisited
ocular treetop vision
evergreen platforms
playful leaf fall

Clouds wander lonely as isolated trees
as Jay's plant seeds of oak,
as all is connected beneath the forest floor

Ideas flow through channels
ride boldly on by
transmitting though forms
through day and through night
a tower of light, corridors of hours,
small and secret thoughts
skyline bower
weathered retreat
a doorway of hope.

Beyond houses and history
into legend and myth
from stone and brick buildings
to moss and feathered heath
with no reprise or concessions
into darkness now,
shot through with flashing light
changing doors
locks and keys
silver bark fingers
root planted feet,
lit spine trunk
breathing life giver

Close to the source
beyond the earthly realms
landscapes forming
through ruined castle walls

Aperture of soft fog light,
distilled grand rime machine,
surrendered spaces time lapse
friends looking out onto a familiar scene
from profane to sacred and back again

Beneath the hills by the secret garden
through the haze of the misty morning
the sun cuts through illuminating
and wakes me gently ruminating
through the woods
into the inner light
out of timeless shadows
towards every dawn

Temple of light in planted lines
circular journey along the same straight path
the law of perplexing returns

Hiding within plain sight
legends of clean landscaping
the centre of purpose
overlooked by passers by
Long straight track
leading to whatever is beyond
younger guardians of older souls
mountainous horizon over clear blue sea
millions of mineral pieces gently underfoot
on the edge of the elements
moving boundaries
changing priorities

Two lovers look across the generations of time
there is a secret hidden in a box
in a fortress
surrounded by a moat
the day will come for the spark to catch light
in the darkness
full of love
sealed with hope

Captured through another lens
escaping memories and aspects
invisible and apparent

known and unknown
liked and otherwise
secret, hidden and public

Quayside contemplation
on a winter afternoon
bright shining reflecting broken waves
vanishing songs of sirens
flight in sight of silence
Stillness

Winter sun dancing in between clouds
sky reflected in shallow pools
abandoned footsteps
washed from time
temporary traces of humanity
dazzled by the transience of a single moment
tidal becoming and going
clay pipe animated wanderings
pictures drawn in sand
erased and redrawn
footsteps are just impressions

What is permanence anyway?

As the world disappears
all forms dissolve
ghost ship sails
walk toward nothingness
lost within cloud
a ghostly retreat
a body made of Oak
in the winter darkness.

How many feet across the years
walked upon these old stone steps
an imprinted memory
at the edge of sight
built from fine Welsh stone
How many souls did aspire above
up to the top and the panorama
the river winds like a silver snake
the hills unfold and communicate.

Hidden depths in earthen womb
from inner earth to windswept hill
by oceans waves and coastal path
where rivers meet and merge
water trickles through the past in stone
forever flowing onwards
fresh water mixing with saline
sailing thoughts and memories
like leaves on a soft breeze
forever changing
dancing and grinning

Saxon moot haunts the font
crystal clear water whispers
ecclesiastical tearoom clatter
painted realities left unfinished
trees standing over epochs,
again and again and again

Tendrils reaching upward
the world turned upside down
the darkness of winter
out of timeless shadows

A whisper of the future
caught within a spell
ancient Egyptian hieroglyphs
in gardened England
genius locorum
spans the modern world.

Winter trees in bud
slowly awakening
as warmth breathe
slowly outwards

small signs of rejuvenation
stone statue standing still
frozen in shadows
frozen in time

Within a secret grove
on the holy island
Isis unveiled as Sulis Minerva
crumbling walls on solid foundations
eternal in spirit through the ages

Modern concrete ancient sites
ceremonial spring celebrations
Bran the Blessed forever vigilant
untold stories of Mother Thames
forever changing and adapting

Cultures colliding
snow dissolves into puddles
walking between worlds and thoughts
Surrealist art cave light
alchemical figures
Song of the Earth

A well-tended garden
looks onto concrete surfaced burial mounds,
ancient societies accomplishments
replaced by grey consumerism
concrete monoliths to capitalism
obscure the horizon
wasted space, with smashed out windows
broken glass and a mosaic of used needles
A makeshift fence apologetically pushed aside
nature more determined than tarmac

This house had another purpose once
a place of charity and safety
now preserved time is its only trade
relics of bygone days
exhibitions of imagination
flints of antiquity
mannequins of sleeping souls

The silence of sleeping stories
bewildered characters playing out roles
illusions of domestic bliss
kitchen sink dramas
under a peaceful sky
birdsong serenades
completing each chapter

Growing ideas through the planting of seeds
worlds from words
progressed from dreams
each idea has its time
brought to life by likeminded thinking
unfolded planted plans uncovered
beneath a painted rolling sky
landscape poems sketched in soil

Mistletoe colonies
as planets around the world tree
leaning on its axis
suspended by air and roots
natural pattern thinking
projected into form

An arboreal sentinel
life-supporting machine
reaching up towards the sun
with feet firmly planted in the ground
Saturn strong, prepared and ready
Jupiter birthing new beginnings

Sentient guardians of the old town
below stairs chamber
containing holy relics
money counting countenance
severed saint's fingers
past tense reverence
holy earth water
over flowing sentiments
bright blue eyes

The first signs of blossom
always give me hope
beautiful intricate blooms suddenly appear
uplifted by such small signs of warmth
on a cold and clear day

I walk in imagination
travel in dreams
listen in silence
swim in infinity
blossom birthing vernal beauty
temporary
some lost bliss of spring

Seat of natural learning
smart thinking syndicates
leaves of historic texts
rivers of consciousness
reflected image in a crystalline pool

Above as below
in an animist theatre
slowly descending sun
dream sleep serenades

Aeons passed with each step
centuries in the length of an arm
decades between fingers
years in millimetres
then back at the same spot I first began
I begin again
changed through time
looking towards infinity

Contrasting halves of the same picture
castles and flooded meadows
pass by in daydream stations
twilight lyrics surround me
swirling as dizzy fruit flies

Restless determination
forgotten on a changing tide
glimpses of Utopia
memorialised with a domed device
call all to the light
from absolute darkness
distant moon-rise
peeking between houses

I follow you
through the Victorian brickwork
through the heavily budded trees
through the roads and traffic
from memory and recollection.
church towers and the passing of time
the view much the same as forever before,
a rainbow beyond over Stinsford Fields
walking through memory
of poetry and prose

unchanging museum
lost childhood love

What is sacred to one person
is mundane to another
what represents life
in all its forms and complexity
what it means to be alive
what it means to feel
what is to be preserved and recorded
what holds value
what defines place

Lost in time
preserved in earth
in the open air
ruinous remains of the day
pedestals supporting air
voids of meaning re-interpreted
photographed to infinity

Silent footsteps muted by moss
birdsong through the filter of leaves
soft breeze and the creaking branches
songs to summon the dusk
twilight in infinity

Green lion eating sunlight
bathed in gold
unseen aquifers flow freely beneath feet
shadow play puppet show

Imagined companions
real within dreams and visions
navigated by stars
reflected in radiant poetry

A sketch of Hendnesburia
dancing dryads in eternity
cross country nostalgic running
strolling in spring shade
symmetry in dendrochronology

Animate Earth
mirrors of the subconscious
all in perfect harmony
vaults of antiquity
on public display

Preserved and presented
stolen away
curated, restated with historic zeal
magical objects related in space

The ghost of MacGregor
and ritual forms
translation of meanings
symbols to words
the esoteric over ground
hidden in plain sight,

Cavernous hall housing block
libraries of knowledge
angles are angels
as once was now
forever is now
all else but now is illusion
the time is now eternal

As the shadows lengthen
the night is but a mile away
follow the moon's journey
through time
all potential within
is expressed outside
a lifetime in one breathe

Searching ever upwards
as sunflowers to sun
for lunar song lines
time standing still

As a picture captured
memory preserved
corrupted by a paper prison

Emerald glow in long dark days
slowly pacing, pulsing, waking
creating light within its husk
shining without question
within, without, above, below, beyond,
unbound.

Vanished in a passing second
perfectly timed journey
focused light chalk reflection
folding fields of patchwork enfolding
the growth of seeds of change

Half light trickles in sleeplessness
the light from within is without
an oasis of eternity
inventing new worlds
from imaginary words

What matters and lasts is still standing
Stories aplenty
hill of memories
crumbled castles
into another world
far removed from here

Receding golden light
day progressing into night
space created to commune
with unveiling otherness
the conjuring of names
the process of becoming

On the edge
views across tomorrow
the future
beyond the horizon
mountains of my mind
landscape of dreams
clouds from tomorrow
float away
surrender to the moments
all is as should be
the dying light of day
a time for reflection

On synchronicity of timing
then long time waiting
joyous celebration
lost in music
fighting through crowds
finding lost love
to a silent cave
the joining of cultures
early start
grey clouds
brightening perspectives

The ancient and almost
as good as anyway
next to glass monoliths
reinvented centres
bright and optimistic
satisfactory functionality
a deep centred solitude
meandering river
by old wise trees
flowing reflections
as the moon reflects the sun

A time of equality and balance
a time when all is made new
a time of light in extension
with all that ever has been
all that ever will be
nothing hidden
banished shadows
division and exclusion
separation and difference
are enemies of equality

All exists in potential
grounds for recovery
new signs of spring
homeopathy health plan
Chelsea pensioner guardians
bowling green best
afternoon teas
political manifestos
planting for peace
To those preserving peace with integrity

At the dawn of spring nature sings
we are all one in essence
I see you coexisting with the busy city
the restless advancement of technology
hurrying for the next place
another transaction

The years move on
the faces change
the shop fronts evolve
from physical to virtual
faces change again
a passing breeze
a voice on the wind
the blink of an eye
built around
preserved in a green idyll
a space of solitude
in an unnatural landscape
Do you remember?

Pollard tree
spring close cut
moon rising,
Libra azimuth

Hengist is that you?

Buried here within
360 degrees of nothing
the uncrowned king
pavement scrawled
sacred texts,
awakening from a long sleep
awakening from darkness to light
awakening from the cold earth
awakening into day from night

Druitt garden Sunday stroll
spring flower canopies
low sun atmosphere
new leaf empire
pathway to yesteryear
silver sculpted bark

Remembering myth
tattooed in tangled branches
another day, a different tree
roots in the same earth
watered by the same rain
breathing the same air
all are connected

Seeds on the breeze
know no boundaries
birds on the wing, soaring free
enveloped in a waterfall of sleep

A haze of tangled half-thoughts
vision on the periphery
reason on the outside
chalk womb earth centre

River source stone marker
avenue to every tomorrow
Sun centred astrology
every word ever written

Craft societies local industry
border village rural bibliography
under a changeable sky
Narcissi bedding surrounds
a clipped neat resting place
Yew tree ancestors
controlled bursts of wildness
cloudless vernal sky
germinating seed thoughts
lightning speed branches
in glacial flow
leaf mould mycelium villages

Interconnected sky poems
Druidic apples in circular groves
red sky promise or warning
within the atmosphere of Mona

Tree lined viewing station
tree house hideout
momentary passing beauty
seven years of solitude
mist scented mountaintops
esoteric landscape maps
gardening perennial weeds
flowering for lifetimes

Hawk circles on horizon lines
aperture to blossom
through entangled thicket
regeneration and simplicity
all necessity and beauty
secret societies
of arts and poetry,

One hundred days of hope
seeds duly planted
travel towards the light
up above the town

Beyond traffic and street sound
against the castle wall
looking upon Priory Hill

Reaching ever upward
hills for rolling down
eclipse the sun with worship
sunrays beaming down

Willows watching rivers running still
reflected sky flowing in reverse
polarised realistic perspectives
dream visitation gardening
sensational beauty
What are you seeking?
What are you searching for?

All is made new
in the spring dawn
flowers and tower blocks
heightened awareness
balcony view of forever

From deep within the earth
iron rich and filtered pure
bird song and passing shadows
elemental tranquillity
family and sharing
remembering and sensing
sat on stone by chalice well

In 1770 these words were carved
scratched into glass
scraped into life
transparency over landscape
thoughts over the world
remembrance in mineral

Into the depths beneath streams of
unconscious consciousness
what once was is now
in new ways
in conversation
memories revealed

Memories of truths and perspectives
versions of yesterday today
strolling down a sun lit street
ending in a welcome retreat

Apple orchards return to life
eternal spring flows without
several meanings to each verse
seven centres beyond words

A silent walk onto the woods
connecting to the earth
through my feet
my attention wanders like a river
my breathing becomes as the tide

Rocks shivering
as vibrating particles
each sounding it's own song
focus onto a particular tree
communication between tree and me

Touch and breath harmonised
sound from my heart
flowing from roots
towards the sky

Slumbering thoughts
molecular activity
a unique expression of this moment
tonal patterns forming
Nature's song.

Each pathway leads onwards
each journey towards tomorrow
each step moving forwards
each breath follows another

Turn over a new leaf for a new season
seed
shoot
leaf
bud
flower
fruit
and the cycle circles again

Simplicity in reaching for the light
without thinking
planning or question
just being, doing, naturally
then meeting
others of like mind
with the same goal
the same why

A moment of kaif
of artistic revelry
lost in music
cultivating form
from thin air

Water reflected
soft sand impressions
vanishing footsteps
like obsolete memories
reformed and buoyant
ready to return
still below the surface forever

Beyond time beautiful reflections
sculpted remembrance of form
cleared memories in earth scraped clean
amnesiac rewarded overgrowth absence
the spirit of futuristic development

Blossoming broken trunk dryad
regeneration of fecund spring
skylines of sentient stone
beneath fast moving troposphere
stages of ages past
forever travelling in cycles

Thought streams within good company
thought forms within animate nature
thoughts of family and all connections
thought cleared and silent speech
thought less and more action
thought forming stream of life
thought as above
thought so below
thought as without
thought so within

Forgotten memorials and retired buildings
parks of remembrance
behind placard scaffold
signs reminding passers by
of a lost landscape

Tidal emotional discoveries,
cloud locked sunshine
occlusion of solar rays
brilliance revealed again
the rarely found thicket
forgotten pathways discovered
above wild coastline
through dense darkness
towards my beginning
almost homeward bound
so near yet far
several strands entwined

Forever rejoice in song
centred in progression
sandwiched in modernity
praised for forward thinking
laughing at dirty jokes
sailing to complexity

beyond grey city sky
in remembrance of life well lived
large family
faith and strength
sometimes solitude
and mystery

I remember kindness
individuality, politics and wine
playing in the old vicarage
running on warm summer grass
sadness and lost years
Church and country
music and song

Looking to dark skies
and sunlit trees
polarity of emotional landscape
bereavement at April's end
advent of the merry month of May
violence of Spring
soliloquy of Summer

All services stood in line
all empty, forgotten
awaiting redevelopment
or maybe destruction
preserved neglected space
void of faded grandeur
utility and function
neighboured by modernity
passed by the transient
everyone heading somewhere
nobody stopping here.

Each day in repetition
an era for every day
presenting change
an epoch of every day in infinity
and infinity of change within a day

an epoch of change within a second
a time for change within the blink of an eye

Industrial dreams of builders
and wreckers of civilisation
habitation, mobilisation and the edge lands
passing through the changing tides
ancient futures in red brick buildings

An arbour of tree lined love
a passageway of becoming who we are
a cycle of ages and agelessness
edible transience
on-going community in infinity
looped with a perfect life-scape of now

Man-made stagnant streams
deserted snake cities and fields
graffiti mural maps
shining with location markers

Cave art optimism
sympathetic magic
ancient byway, well-trod track
stone row alignment
safe free movement
inward journeying
above Blake's abode
a changing skyline
vertically ascended progress
leading nowhere new
old ground covered
loved and rediscovered

Every year in May
the background for a photograph
flowering pink azalea growing
in time with me

A walk to the top of the world
azure blue and seamless sky blending
slow floating mist arising
all life and death
in the blink of an eye

Seed thoughts hatching
language forming
cliff fallen fossils
cocooned in clay

Burial ground imprints
Neolithic place markers
Bronze Age spaceships
Iron Age incubators
modern day curiosities
present tense poems

Deep within the language of trees
future, present and past written
roots and branches feeding dreams
lifetime of soul nature study
unfolding fields and rippled coastline

Walking on the edge of worlds
merging elements in alchemical mist
friendship connection and earth
time stood still and quiet

as resigned as we are to this moment

Several spines aligning
groves of hidden secrets
found and finding peace
pieces coming together
joining, coupling embracing
several worlds colliding
fire walk with me

Lines of productive thought
as far as the eye can see
ahead and around the curve
looking across the valley
potential in sleeping
fecundity in streams
thirst fed through melting ice

Re-imagining lost landscapes
childhood paths and footprints
distant time rewarded
peace found unexpectedly

An ancient and familiar face
the watcher from the crosses
the face of a tomb forgotten
the face of the Bach of sand
the face of the untied knot
the face encased in stone
carved in stone
set in stone

the face reveals forever

Roads to and from family history,
form formal and informal processions
cycles of life and death
chants, songs and memories

Hill top tree covered in the round
hometown turf
home time trees
climbed as a child
looked out from
cocooned within
homeward bound and found again

What doesn't change?
What remains the same?

That which time can never alter

Love and hope throughout world
a step towards unity and light
Love, Love is all there is
all we have
all we need

Light streaming through stained glass stories
memorial carvings for Steinulf the priest
Axon tomb exhibition centre
absorbed stone and wooden memory

Life goes on and the sun still shines
people come together beneath the open sky
new friendships form
but no one is forgotten
the spirit lives on through the unbroken chain

Of childhood dreams
of teenage ambitions
all humanity of hope
each blossom a sigil of nature
each flower picture of potential

unfolded perfection

Across the water is the future,
reimagined networks of joined up thinking
an ark of musical healing
beneath the billowed boughs
above the warm stable earth
breathing the fragrant fresh air

Love, truthfulness and wisdom
and the spaces in between
Tall and strong
houses and buildings below

Swaying gently, great heights
playing my own whispered music
casting mottled shade
across distances of time

Watching and observing
feeling and sensing
dreaming in branches
in leaves as receptors

Complementing the illusion
of bright blue sky
visible and real
deepening relationships
elements and sound

Tobias in my heart
the wanderer returns
soft scratch sunrise
faint call for home
eleven am, third of June
one last goodbye
one last grace
an empty vessel
a moon temple
fixed in space
a full heart
missing your presence
last embrace
body returned to earth

sweet peaceful friend
until we meet again
travelling dream companion

A beautiful vision of regeneration
naturalistic self seeding planting
restoration with a modern twist
pathways of plant paradise
if only life were so simple
I sometimes think

So many familiar faces
friendships preserved through time
the happiness of remembrance
the loss of youth
the beauty now
of being together

Encouragement and kindness
a thousand floating golden suns
constellations of swaying seed
living breathing green and gold
now I'm looking outwards to tomorrow
inwards to yesterday
the meeting of elements
the merging of memories
the surprise of déjà vu

Following my own path
uncovering undiscovered castles
fortresses of the unknown
fields of fortitude
and the ever-changing sky
whistle stop full stop
space to wait
to breath
to sit
to begin again

On boarding
oncoming towards something
change is paramount
reflected group reflections
simple ripple light reflection
light wave pathway
taking stock of ideas
writing down titles of books
letting go of identity
giving myself space

Arboreal standing rows
planted dryad storytellers
time passing over the yardarm

the subtle shingle soundtrack
liminal light poetry hour
Across speckled fields
of every single thought and idea
each presenting itself
in the gentle breeze

Options passed or unnoticed
circling the next cycle will come
long views for cyclical time
fields of travelling shapes

Inhabited longitude of song
clothed with fresh vigour
new shoots and leaves
meadows in the approaching midsummer
a neighbourhood of networks
each feeding and giving to the other
inland mermaid story telling tavern
nesting bird balconies of sound

Memories lie
betwixt each and every cobble
shadows protect the past
the sun represents reality
becoming no thing, letting go

Now is the dawn, the cultivation of expression
of preservation, of enlightenment
the development of the mind
cultivating presence
corridors of timelessness
horticultural heterodoxy
sensual scent scene
a piece of peace.

Ancient souls whisper in the wind
growing and governing in groves
connected and connecting community
beyond nature is not a thing
everything is nature after all

Yet towers rise as trees
they do not supersede
yet mimic and follow,
brick bark and hollow
a womb, room and tomb
pathway leading ever onwards
at each apparent horizon
begins each turn and choice
each step and breath
leading and leaning
inwards

Rainbow roses in heavenly scented arcs
Venus growing from Saturn's stable base
silver reflected by liquid moonlight
the sky spins in a tuneful tube of light
highlighted angles from mathematical angels
landscape dreaming forevermore
sky gazing scrying school
nature written as poetry
Earth as a foundation
words with hidden meaning
telegraph post alignments
power station lay lines

Gardens of love
gardens of strength
gardens of remembrance
garden for writing
gardens of transcendence
gardens in desolation
gardens of restoration
a garden in my heart

The rewilding of self
solutions for regeneration
after all seemed lost
woodland walks and river swimming
love and peace and balance

Walking through fields of new encounters
walking and thinking
walking and dreaming
singing the songs of summer
river crossing with Penny and Eve
walking talking philosophy tour
everything matters and nothing matters
nothing exists and everything exists
nothing matters and everything matters
There is no authority but yourself?
There is no authority but nature.

Each wave a thought
each leaf an idea
each reflection a reality

Nightingales singing sonnets of sunlight
submit to summer sun somnolence
tree topped tales of territory
language of migration to come
lost days in rapturous music
lost friends
notes floating through air

Cobbled memories
sweat infused walls
school of music
when music was all

Out of the red brick tower
open landscape panoramic view
beyond the edge of nowhere
swim on the scented breeze
raising energies from collective wisdom
sequential sky golden flow
glow golden-lit skies above
reflecting and connecting us

Rolling hills and valleys
circling soaring swifts
days of fun and friendship
nights of dream filled bliss
tress framed by wood from trees
through to emerald fields

Fast moving cloud-forms
nightmares of a silent spring
clearest water, flowing freely
neither unchanged nor unchanging
unchangeable or past remaining
several dozen steps but not to heaven
steps to a hilltop tree lined haven
childhood to adulthood
through learned topography

Into fiction
fiction as life,
life is not fiction
it can be story
history is myth
myth as legend,
myth and legend as truth
life as art, art as life

Beach scene life being
What is truth?
What is truth to you?

Glowing landscape at midnight
in the light of a supermoon
juniper fruit flow
truth and commonality
Elvis ecosystem
circle of truth
circle of trust
reverberations of one truth
rivulets of flowing ideas
rivers pulsing, running onward
righteous militant feminist dream
just in time

Looking out to an unknown future
the invisible end point
or a prescient present
all are open
thousands of tiny moments
reflected mirrors
on transient waves

Clotted clouds
tonal greys
each masked memory
distant islands
land locked illusion
anthropological folklore,

Nature reclaiming the streets
a re-accruing vision of renewal
Asphalt rewilded walkways
crumbling brickwork temples
dreams of Pan
leaf shelter security
Pythagorean tree trajectory
circular rooted light
nature as cure
UFO's in back gardens
each with a camera
little sign of nature
many signs of human nature
many sides of life

Occulted desired retail
suspended first editions
esoteric passageway
shop front carnival
long lost logic

Layers of language
layers of meaning
layers of existence
layers of earth
layers of perspective

The sun shines on all
there is only light without darkness
darkness is an illusion
the sun always shines

Night and day are relative
to where we are in relation to where the sun is
at any given moment in time

Alien landscape
and manmade impositions
alien landscape and manmade gardens
beacons light for elemental sisters
windswept-pebbled fingerprints
tunnels of light, gold and green
living green of the heart
gold of the sun surrounding
over and above
Into Now Here
triangular traversing space travel
beneath living skies
above living water
along breathing pathways
toward the endless shining stars

Rural flatlands to organic haven
the road to the city of industry
city of culture
city of memories
city of today
back to nature and the coast
back to eve
to the edge
back to roads reclaimed by nature
by lives transformed by migrating birds
to preserving all that matters
washing away what isn't needed
age, experience and youth
hand in hand in hand

Organic regeneration through seasons
soulful stirring of chaos
southerly wind song lines
helping hands land alliance
shares in future food
taste of once again
oasis of live fields
happily returning songbirds
butterfly palace glasshouse
the corridors of my mind
the corridors of distant memory space
projecting into future times and sounds
the light within and at the end of the tunnel

This place, there are aspirations here
these aspirations are clear,
achieving them how near?

Glass like abstract mind reflection
changed through experience
is there one turning point, one only
is each moment in time a point of change
each moment an opportunity
if only we can be present

Riverside holistic habitat as home
meditation of liquid sound sources
meandering instant composition musical
choirs of creatures heard but not seen
creaking branch percussion accompaniment
into nothing and everything
from tomorrow to today
how to stop time
when to stop time, reasons to stop time
reasons to stay alive, reasons to stop time
reasons to stay alive, reasons to love
reasons to live.

Sometimes the walls close in
the light is restricted
the view is obscured
the future unclear
and feeling far way
then the briefest glimpse of light
of everything opening up
the mirror wiped clean
the diamond vehicle
dark clouds can gather
the sun still shines through
the contrast of light and dark
a gathering of thoughts

Summer soliloquy of regeneration
many faces of ancient sun worship
meeting old friends through time
early harvest season commences
warm and relaxed evenings
passing thoughts and seasons

Into the deep, the city's synapses
those hidden depths, history in feet
rediscovered past lives, sinking slowly down

Souls rising steadily upwards
to the castle top through layers of time
specks of grain generations
lives led and recorded
red house ancient archives
Spickernell and Druitt dreams
geologic roads of progress
aural history adult school
Brigid's rising cyclic song
life reflected in a
transient dance of the light
all beauty in a wingspan stretch
all music in the sounds of now
from a higher place everything is changed

All is relative and connected
all is one without separation
a single thought community
an ideal of a society
a flight in mind, a mind in flight

Grandiose gestures and exuberant taste
obsolete and empty, a museum of loss

Soaring across and through
all is patchwork borders
traversed senseless division

All is made new, all is ever one
at this point there is no separation
with this view all is connected
not only temporary perspective
underlying truth in essence
mountains of ambition
streams of consciousness
infinite horizons

Will this path lead anywhere?
All paths lead somewhere,
new realms of the known and unknown,
centre of the city of mind
centre through time
centre for peace, all are welcome
centre for reconciliation
centre of love, surrounded by commerce
haven of silent thought
centre of self, inner journeying
outer word working, much loved peace

Closed off footpaths
hidden footprints
flowing stream
lapping waves
wild byway

Post-industrial beauty
walking through the city looking up
then atop Arthur's Seat looking out

Climbing strata's, feeling free
from bright blue skies
into the underworld
breath trails and plays
of the fading light
then all is infinite darkness

Open-eyed womb meditations
a stopped moment in time
welcoming the returning light
awaking dreams of multi-dimensional worlds
subterranean learning spaceship
a line of purpose bordering the familiar
the edge and the visible reflection
solution thinking collective feeling
worlds are colliding in time

From ruins can come great things?
The cyclic tide continues on
a new vision of days to come
horizon line mood enhancer
division and unification
cyclical physical reality
sounds of the sea
songs of the sirens
pebbles on the beach

Each thought made manifest
remembering journeys like these
familiar scents and sounds
friends that feel like old times
new times and sci-fi finds
now times as good as ever

Train track testament terminal
blue-sky time flies
each facing the sun
all made of stars
across aeons of time
I return to home

Into timeless shadows again
walking around in circles
stone sentinels of Lamorna
dancing forevermore
to a tune made of minerals

Three generations of life before me
the cat queen watcher through time
settled on land farming solidity
working in cycles of life
lost and found
secrets in plain view

Rediscover forgotten beauty
full bloom late summer
restored life and love
fair weather kitten sat on windowsill
bathing in late summer sun
boats birthed from umbilical harbour
rock-pooling children discovering life,

Cloudscapes painted on the sky
constellation mirrored sundial
quartz block centred being
needle of stone Om
Boscawen-Un time travelling
joining of migration lines
station of Gorsedd poets
seasons of ritual year
shape and form
interpretation of nature
working in natural conjunction
the artists garden

Sculpted pagan poetry
Bardic-bronzed forms

Rainforest weather machine
walking the canopy
worldwide biome
Kaolin miracle world

The silence of the city
England sweet England
empathy incarnate in time and space
when the music's over
listen more carefully

The same sun shines on every wave
day-lit tunnel, with light shining from within
a rainbow light spectrum
filtered through ferns
Boleigh centred rock
and damp earth cocoon
in the present within
making music from dreams

Gazing into rock-pools
breathing in and out with tidal pulses
reflected sky plant swaying
micro-life landscape continents
ice cold toes warming hearts
viewing Creeg Tol, across to Boscawen-Un
heather and scrubland
hidden reverse fields
crystal flowing quartz
abstract mind maps
conjoining of lines
heaven and earth

Lunar tears on glass sash window
travel on the wind weather system
Last quarter moon
Gemini and Virgo
element of water in Autumn beginning

I have walked to the edge
Albion at the end or beginning
Atlantic tides over hidden Atlantis
myths over mass
facts only serve folklore
cliff and the shadows
threnody to tape deck holidays
passing pylons of the past
lost children found again

Perfection in asymmetric hemispheres
Myelin thought forms as electric ghosts
rise above the landscape
in which I move
moved by the territory
painting patterns
stone saint way marker
stone cross spirit
crossroads shaped T
stone crossroad of faith

Low lit dark lanes
walking in the gloaming
creatures of the wood
waxing quarter moon
twilight animist arboreal architects
clouds of leaf floating
double rainbow doting
twilight encroaching
sleep pattern oaks

From above the roads
are enveloped with leaves and branches
the tarmac snakes only
visible from ground level
Ballardian wilderness
barely kept at bay
I welcome the weeds through the tarmac

Rediscovered pathways to the wooden heart
leaf rustling wind symphonies
of yesterday's weather
foretelling of all that is to come
if we could but hear
enchanting dancing light
under-lit glow forms

Streaming shining pulse
golden dawn arising
the pipers keep the dance moving
sentinels in sound forever
Lamorna melodies on land
living and breathing stories
passed down through generations

Loved and lost and loved again
beneath the understory
seedlings to maturity
cloud seeding harvest
the promise of rain
three hundred years
of the supernal mother
bright autumn days of vision
the crisping leaves
the cycles of time
towards black angels
resurgence of a golden dawn

When poetry is food and wine
then stillness speaks
time slows down
breathing in and out
breath as time enough

When poetry is meditation
when wellbeing of all is considered
alternatives present themselves
faith is not religion
doctrine dissolves
and love is all there is

There is a place where secrets lie
the stripping away of shadows
standing naked with nothing to hide
the harvest of the soul
the joy of the harvest
removal of all illusion
nothing obscured

Stained glass folk art reminders
replicating nature in Portland stone
serving a higher purpose
into the womb
of the theatre of dreams
from equinox to solstice
in the blink of an eye
entering darkness to discover light
meeting old friends
mapping possible futures

Thames side skating
near perpetual motion,
resting revolutions
peaceful protest
sun reflecting joy
friendship rekindled
Autumn walking
the cities expanse
habitat threatened species
here stands the alien
ocean metal warriors
harvesting wind song
spinning blade horizon
windmills of my mined
energy from the air

Yew berries emerging shine brightly
gaps between branches of thought
sacred ground developed around us
thousands of years for one thought
from you
to Yew
and you to I
light flows through
Yew and you and I

The passage of time and time (less) time
passing through the Rubicon
light rippled tide
landscaped skies
wooden heart boat
close to home
the last days of meaning
of love and labour
map and territory
clay and art

Cold receivership
shelves for sale
imminent loss
vultures circling
concrete nothing, discount culture
to sail across the sea
and enter the horizon
disappear from the familiar
to become invisible
floating on waves of sound

An ending of sorts, new breath beginning
singing cyclic songs
of innocence and experience
the nous to see
across aeons of time
the monad in flight
with balanced breath
create circle of light
centred in brow
tongue of flame
through seven centres
with detached view
the expanded universe
into no thing
connected to everything

egress

to new beginnings.

Photos

Seagull in Christchurch, Devon

Schumacher College in Dartington, Devon

Near to Badbury Ring, Dorset

Seagulls in Poole, Dorset

The Edge, Alderley Edge, Cheshire

Poole Harbour, Dorset

Machynlleth, Wales

Timsbury, Hampshire

Christchurch, Devon

Christchurch, Devon

Bowness On Windermere, Lancashire

Montacute House, Somerset

Christchurch, Devon

Saint Buryan, Cornwall

Sandbach, Cheshire

Tobias in Christchurch, Dorset

Christchurch, Dorset

Bransford, Worcester

Rye Harbour, Sussex

Land's End, Cornwall

Boscawen-Un, Cornwall

Lamorna, Cornwall

Anglesey, Wales

Holyhead, Anglesey

Christchurch, Dorset

Stairs to St Giles Hilltop, Winchester, Hampshire

A forgotten doorway

Christchurch, Dorset

The Nine Stones of Winterbourne Abbas

About the Author

Matthew Shaw is a Dorset based composer, musician, and artist who has been releasing music since 2000 under his own name and as Tex La Homa.

He has a love of nature, ancient sites and walking, often with a camera, notepad or recording device to hand. Some of these travels have resulted in the albums *Lamorna*, *Venus Rosalia*, *Fowey* and *Lodge Hill*, combining recordings on site with composition and photography. He has previously self-published three photography books of ancient sites in Britain, and two short volumes of poetry. His music explores the possibilities of the spaces between post-rock, drone music and soundscapes.

Matthew recently worked with Shirley Collins on her new album *Heart's Ease* combining landscape, folk song and field recording.

For more information about Matthew Shaw, with links to his writings, photography and music, please visit **Annwyn House** online: annwynhouse.weebly.com

www.ingramcontent.com/pod-product-compliance
Lightning Source LLC
Chambersburg PA
CBHW071250070526
44583CB00017B/2401